No Matter What Happens

A Story for Children
When Secondary Infertility Happens

Cathie Quillet, LMFT
Illustrated by Jayden Ellsworth

Published by Orange Hat Publishing 2020
ISBN 978-1-64538-137-2

Copyrighted © 2020 by Cathie Quillet
All Rights Reserved
No Matter What Happens: A Story for Children When
Secondary Infertility Happen
Written by Cathie Quillet, LMFT
Illustrated by Jayden Ellsworth

All Rights Reserved. Written permission must be secured from the publisher to use or reproduce any part of this book, except for brief quotations in critical reviews or articles.

For information, please contact:

Orange Hat Publishing
www.orangehatpublishing.com
Waukesha, WI

*For Julia,
and all the other boys and girls who would make
the best big brothers and big sisters.*

Mommy and Daddy said that they want to have another baby. Mommy said that the baby is going to grow super big and that I'll get to teach the baby a lot of things I have already learned. They said, "No matter what happens, our family will always be perfect, just the way we are."

Mommy and Daddy said that when the baby comes, I am going to be a big sister. I am so excited! They said the baby will be a part of our family forever and that we can play dress-up and do art projects together. Mommy and Daddy said, "No matter what happens, our family will always be perfect, just the way we are."

Mommy and Daddy told Nana and Papa that they are going to have another grandchild. They said that they are really excited and that they will always love me and the new baby just the same. I already love the baby so much!
Nana said, "No matter what happens, our family will always be perfect, just the way we are."

We are still waiting on the baby. Waiting is really hard. I have a lot of great stuff to teach the baby, like playing make-believe. Mommy said that the waiting will make me strong and brave even though it is really, REALLY hard. She hugged me and said, "No matter what happens, our family will always be perfect, just the way we are."

Mommy and Daddy have gone to a lot of doctors' appointments lately. I am really getting frustrated. They said that this doctor will help us have a new baby. "I hope it happens really soon," I told Daddy. Daddy said, "Me too, but don't forget that no matter what happens, our family will always be perfect, just the way we are."

Mommy and Daddy said that they wanted to have another baby. I waited and waited. I started preschool and then kindergarten and then waited some more. I wondered if it would ever happen. I could tell that they were getting tired of waiting just like me but that they were also practicing being strong. Mommy and Daddy said, "No matter what happens, our family will always be perfect, just the way we are."

Mommy and Daddy said that we might not be able to have another baby. They squeezed me really tight, and we were all sad for a little bit. I told them, "It is hard to wait, but you are teaching me to be strong. Don't ever forget that no matter what happens, our family is perfect, just the way we are."

8 Tips For Parents Dealing With Secondary Infertility

1) Acknowledge that secondary infertility is infertility. Allow yourself to grieve your diagnosis and this season.

2) Secondary infertility is a balancing act between being a partner in your relationship, being a parent, and being an individual in the difficult season of waiting. Each of these roles is emotionally demanding. Prioritize time to be present for all three.

3) Practice self-care. What made you come alive before you were a mother?

4) When you date your partner, try to put a pin in conversations around parenting and infertility. Focus on enjoying your relationship.

5) Find a support group or a therapist that can help you navigate your emotions.

6) Enjoy your child as an only child. Ideally, they won't carry that title for much longer.

7) Allow yourself to make boundaries on behalf of your mental health when you need to.

8) Seek support from The Quillet Institute. We have coaching packages, online support resources, and books to help you through this difficult season.

Visit us at www.thequilletinstitute.com

THE QUILLET INSTITUTE

Empowering Waiting Parents To Thrive During Infertility

The Quillet Institute educates and empowers waiting parents through:

- One-on-one coaching customized to your needs
- Peace (In)Fertility - An eight-session online video program to help you live well in your wait
- Books, workbooks and other resources written by our CEO Cathie Quillet, Licensed Marriage and Family Therapist

www.thequilletinstitute.com

www.ingramcontent.com/pod-product-compliance
Lightning Source LLC
Chambersburg PA
CBHW041638040426
42449CB00022B/3497